For my dad, Charles H. Weidner,
who taught me about the seasons on the farm
—K.W.Z.

For the Lamonts in Half Moon Bay
—P.L.

THIS IS A BORZOI BOOK PUBLISHED BY ALFRED A. KNOPF

Text copyright © 2014 by Kathleen Weidner Zoehfeld
Jacket art and interior illustrations copyright © 2014 by Priscilla Lamont
All rights reserved. Published in the United States by Alfred A. Knopf, an imprint of Random House Children's Books,
a division of Random House, Inc., New York.
Knopf, Borzoi Books, and the colophon are registered trademarks of Random House, Inc.
Visit us on the Web! randomhouse.com/kids
Educators and librarians, for a variety of teaching tools, visit us at RHTeachersLibrarians.com
Library of Congress Cataloging-in-Publication Data
Zoehfeld, Kathleen Weidner.
Secrets of the seasons : orbiting the sun in our backyard / Kathleen Weidner Zoehfeld ; illustrated by Priscilla Lamont.
p. cm
Summary: "Over the course of a year, a family learns about the role of the sun in the changing seasons"—Provided by publisher.
ISBN 978-0-517-70994-8 (trade) — ISBN 978-0-517-70995-5 (lib. bdg.) — ISBN 978-0-307-98240-7 (ebook)
[1. Seasons—Fiction. 2. Sun—Fiction.] I. Lamont, Priscilla, illustrator. II. Title.
PZ7.Z715Sek 2014
[E]—dc23    2013021351
The illustrations in this book were created using pen and watercolors.
MANUFACTURED IN MALAYSIA
April 2014    10 9 8 7 6 5 4 3 2 1    First Edition
Random House Children's Books supports the First Amendment and celebrates the right to read.

# Orbiting the Sun in Our Backyard

# Secrets
## OF THE
# Seasons

by KATHLEEN WEIDNER ZOEHFELD

illustrated by PRISCILLA LAMONT

Alfred A. Knopf 🐕 New York

I can see just about everything from up here in my tree house. But my friend Zack noticed something I didn't. Something really big! The sun is setting earlier than it did just a few weeks ago.

Everyone says that the sun "rises" in the morning and "goes down" in the evening, but really it's the *earth* that's moving. We have sunrise and sunset because the earth is spinning.

It's easy to think that every day should be exactly half dark and half light. But Zack's right. Our daylight time is getting shorter. I love the long, warm days of summer. Shorter days mean it'll soon be getting cooler. Autumn is on its way!

After Zack heads for home, I lie flat on the grass and try to feel the earth spinning like a giant blue top, tilting and twirling through the blackness of space.

My stomach feels floppy. Maybe all this spinning *is* making me dizzy. Or maybe it's because I know the summer's ending. Maybe it's because school starts *tomorrow*!

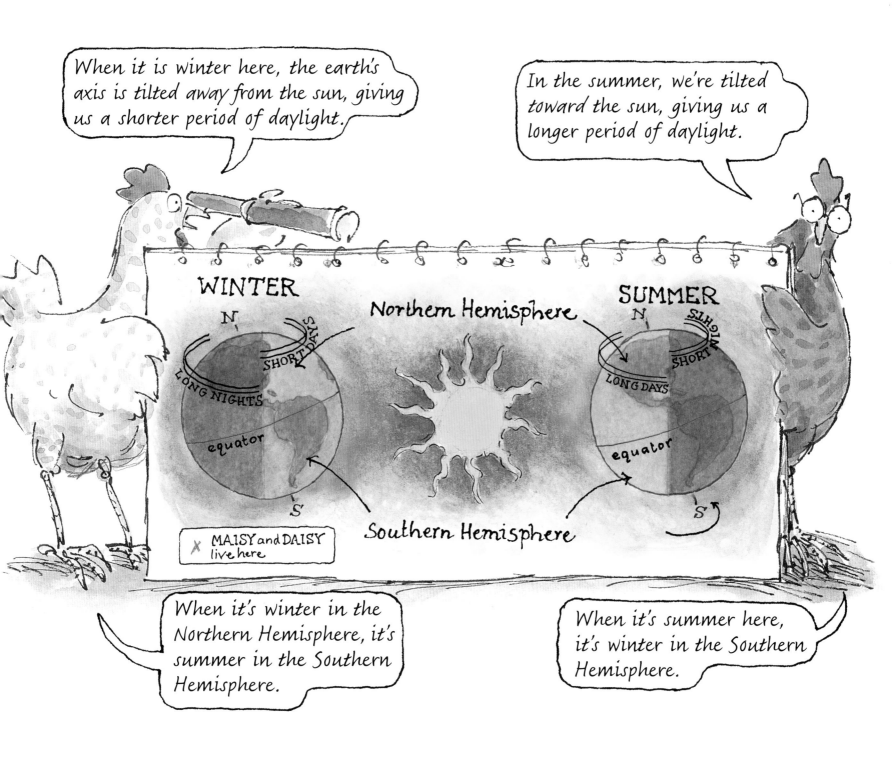

Every day, as soon as that school bus gets us home, Zack and I toss off our shoes and hit the ground running. But one day in late September, the grass stops feeling friendly to our feet. It's cold, and it makes our toes ache.

## Autumnal (or Fall) Equinox

September 22 or 23. On this day, the number of hours of daylight equals the number of hours of darkness.

At this point, the earth's axis is not tilting toward or away from the sun. If you were standing on the equator at noon, the sun would be directly over your head.

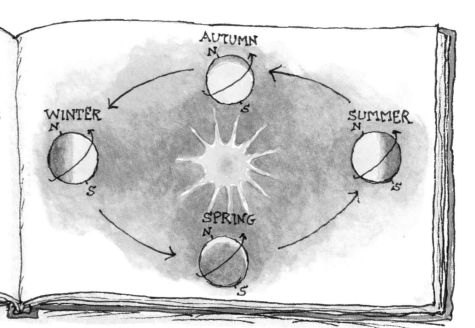

Autumn brings all sorts of new things to notice. A squirrel bounces along a bare branch. All around us, the leaves are changing. When the cool wind blows, the colors fly—red and yellow, copper and gold.

As the leaf curtain falls, it shows us a secret—a twig nest in the branches. It's empty now.

It looks like the geese are pointing the way for the other birds to follow!

Wait for me. I'm coming with you!

Up above, a giant V of geese heads south. *Ka-ronk, ka-ronk!* they call. I wonder if the small birds have flown off, too.

Some scientists say that birds have little "compasses" in their heads that tell them which way south is.

That's no surprise! Birds are extremely intelligent. Not only do some of us have built-in brain compasses, but we also understand the changing position of the sun and can memorize the patterns of the stars. Migrating birds use that information to help them find north and south as well.

They're so vain. Chickens do not migrate!

Soon the leaves have all flown away with the birds. The days have been growing shorter–and quieter, too. At sundown, we hear only the scritchy-scratch of a few last katydids arguing, high in the treetops–*katy-did, katy-didn't, katy-did, katy-didn't.*

Then one day they are silent, too.

We can't stay in the tree house very long now. The cold wind makes the branches rattle and shake.

Before we know it, the sun is gone and the trees stand like black skeletons against a silvery sky.

# Winter Solstice

December 21 or 22. On this day, there are fewer daylight hours than on any other day in the year. From now on, the daylight hours will slowly be getting longer and longer.

The North Pole is tilted away from the sun.

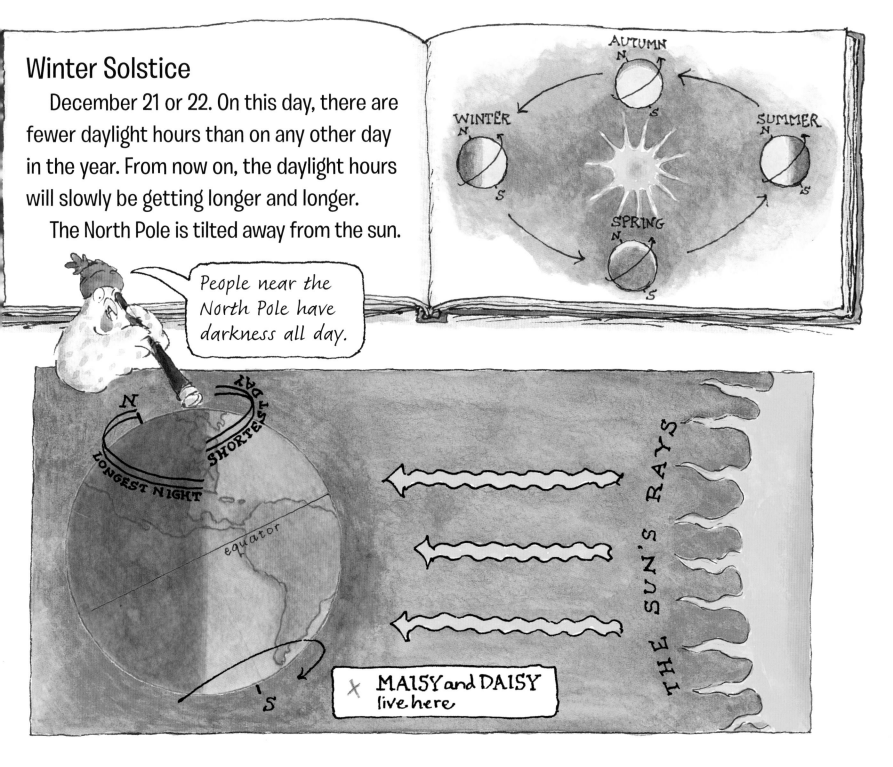

We snuggle up inside and eat our supper by candlelight.

I think about the geese and the other migrating birds. By now they must be lounging around someplace warm, like Jamaica.

Jamaica is much closer to the equator than we are. It's *always* warm near the equator.

The next morning, we wake up to a whirl of white!

When the snowfall stops, I shoosh up to the tree house for a better look. The world is hushed. Four chickadees huddle together on a branch, their feathers all fluffed up. I'm glad they've decided to stay.

Every morning, I set out new seeds. The winter birds flock around— even the shy cardinals. They need all the food they can get in this weather!

I don't see many animals out and about. But crisscrossing the snowy fields, the tracks of fox and mouse, deer and grouse tell mysterious tales.

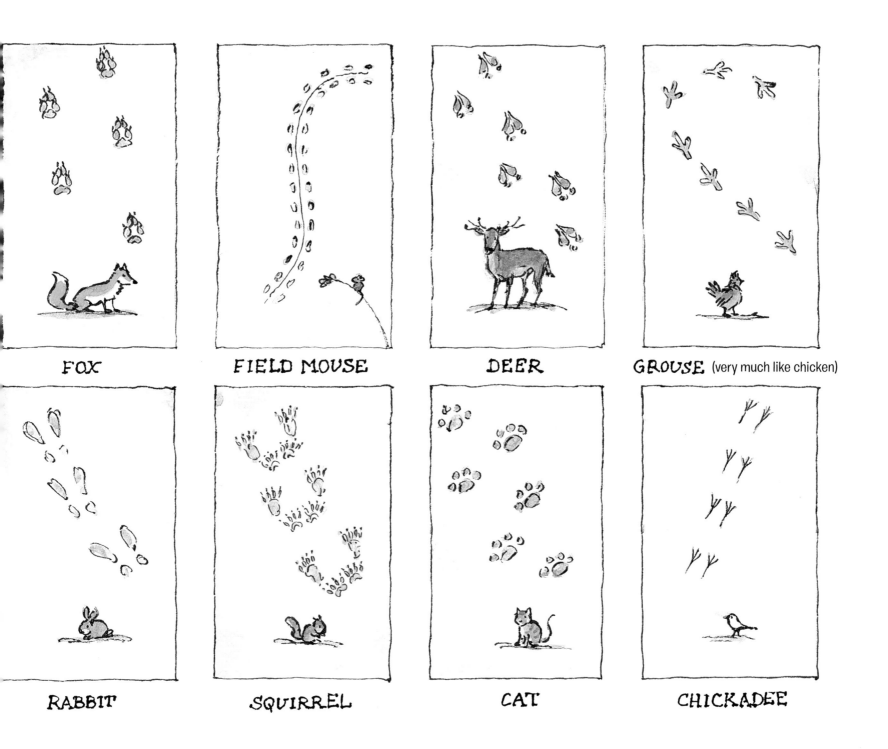

FOX

FIELD MOUSE

DEER

GROUSE (very much like chicken)

RABBIT

SQUIRREL

CAT

CHICKADEE

# Winter Birds

stay here and forage
or hunt for food

chickadee

blue jay

hawk

grouse

cardinal

# Migrating Birds

fly to warmer places with plenty of food in the
winter months, then return again in the spring

swallow

robin

northern oriole

Canada goose

Arctic tern

As the chilly winter weeks pass, I begin to notice the days getting longer. It's hard to tell, but it's true. I wonder if the animals know it, too.

Overhead, the geese are returning. *Ka-ronk, ka-ronk!* they cry. I know the other birds will be right behind them.

In the garden, Pete's the first to see the purple and yellow crocuses pushing through the melting snow.

Up in the tree house, I see tiny green buds on the branches.

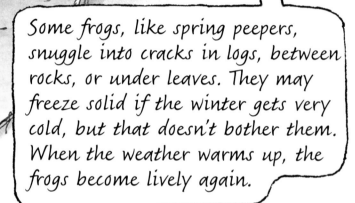

During the coldest part of the winter, frogs hibernate. Bullfrogs move down to the cold, cold water at the bottom of their pond. They become very sluggish. They do not need to eat. They take in what little oxygen they need through their skin.

Some frogs, like spring peepers, snuggle into cracks in logs, between rocks, or under leaves. They may freeze solid if the winter gets very cold, but that doesn't bother them. When the weather warms up, the frogs become lively again.

One evening, a robin touches down on a branch and sings to the sunset-*cheer up, cheerily, cheer up!* Spring has arrived!

Tonight when I go to bed, I'll leave my window open so I can smell the warm, damp earth. I'll fall asleep to the sound of spring peepers calling down by the pond.

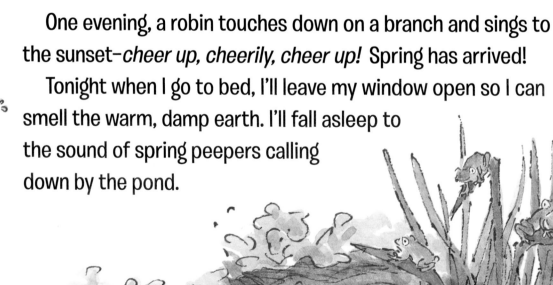

## Vernal (or Spring) Equinox

March 20 or 21. On this day, once again, the number of hours of daylight equals the hours of darkness.

As on the autumnal equinox, the sun is directly above the equator.

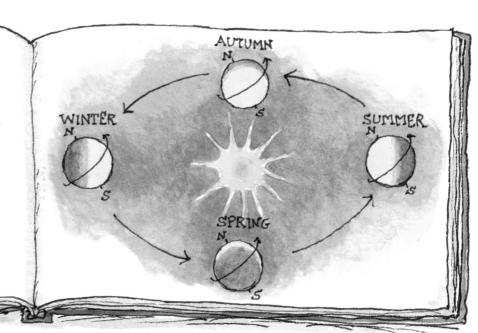

Each morning now, the bird chorus sings me awake.

Zack and I notice a pair of robins gathering twigs and flying them up to a branch.

As we watch the robins working and the new leaves growing, I think I can actually feel the earth speeding along its path in space.

Our tree house is a spaceship! It may *seem* like it's always in the same place-right up in the old maple tree. But really, it's zooming us around the sun-spinning us toward the summer.

By the time the last day of school rolls around, my feet feel trapped in my shoes. I can't wait to wiggle my toes in the warm grass again. I want to smell flowers in the air!

Finally, school's out and we're free!

This evening Zack's family comes over for supper. My dad and mom barbecue, and we eat outside, under the maple tree.

As darkness falls, a thousand fireflies light up the lawn—fireworks to celebrate the coming of summer!

Everybody at school today was cheering, "It's summer!"

It's almost summer.

We creep quietly up to the tree house now. The maple leaves, broad and green, hide a new secret. A breeze lifts the leaves, and we see the robin family, tending their chicks. The mother and father fly back and forth with worms. The babies' beaks are wide open and waiting.

## Summer Solstice

June 20 or 21. On this day, there are more daylight hours than on any other day in the year.

Now the North Pole is tilted *toward* the sun.

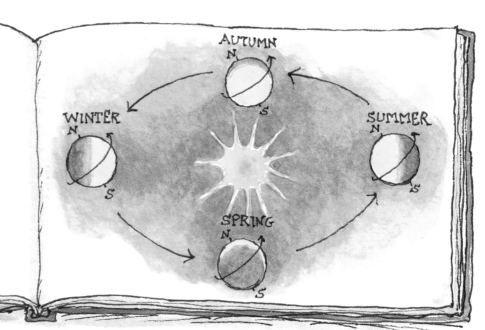

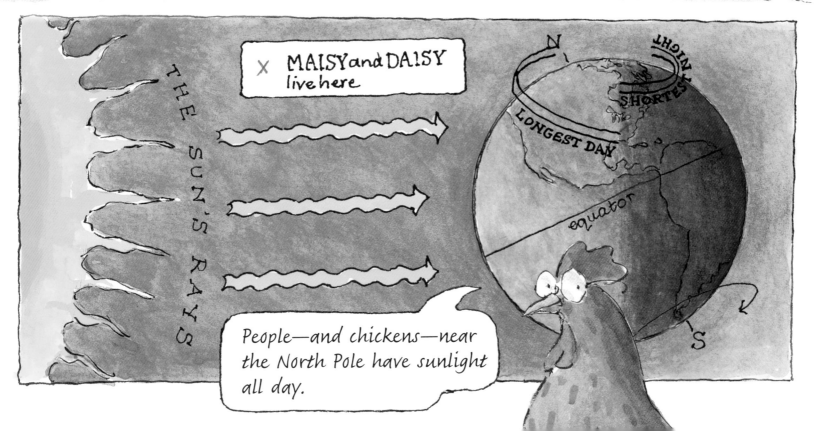

x MAISY and DAISY live here

THE SUN'S RAYS

LONGEST DAY

SHORTEST NIGHT

equator

People—and chickens—near the North Pole have sunlight all day.

Some days the sun is *so* hot, even the squirrels droop.

On the laziest afternoons of summer, we stretch out near the pond and watch the dragonflies darting. We dangle our feet in the water, and small fish brush against our toes.

When the steamy wind blows, maple seeds whirligig past our tree house like crazy rain.

I know the days are getting shorter again, even though it doesn't feel like it yet. The animals must know it, too. They race to raise their babies before the cold weather returns.

I like to fish.

By summer's end, the robin babies have learned how to find worms for themselves.

I've learned a few things, too. This time the signs of autumn don't escape me. In fact, I've been looking forward to watching them all.

As we ride our spaceship on its steady course around the sun, it will soon carry us back to school. And we'll all travel together-back through another autumn, winter, spring, and summer-back through the cycle of the seasons.